NEW ENGLAND COOKING

Kate Cranshaw

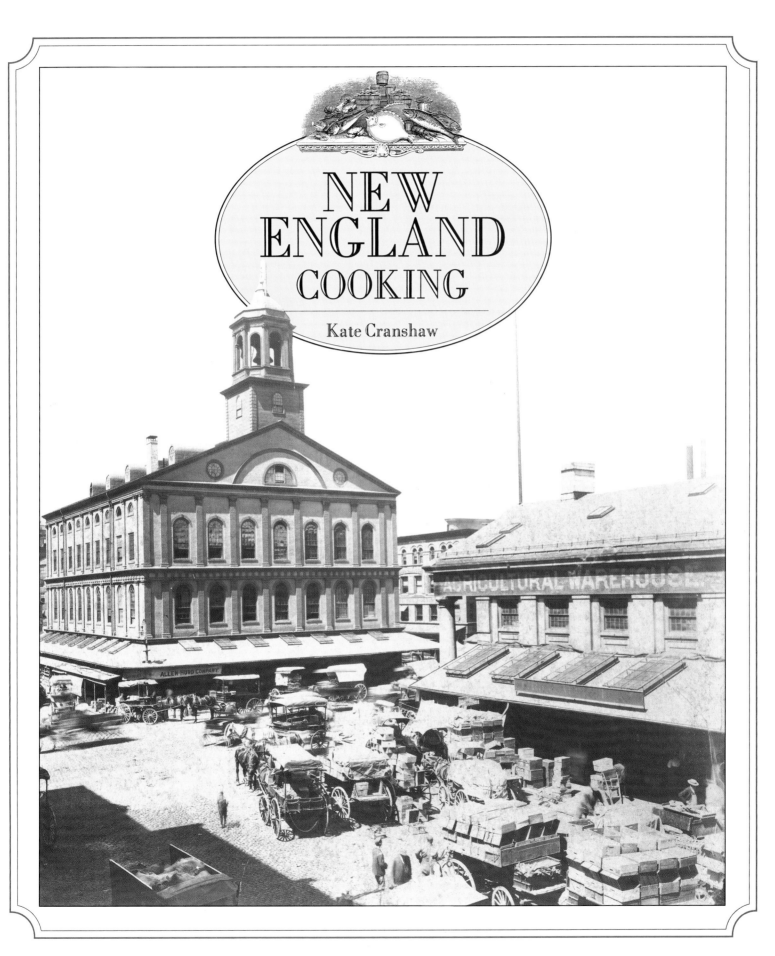

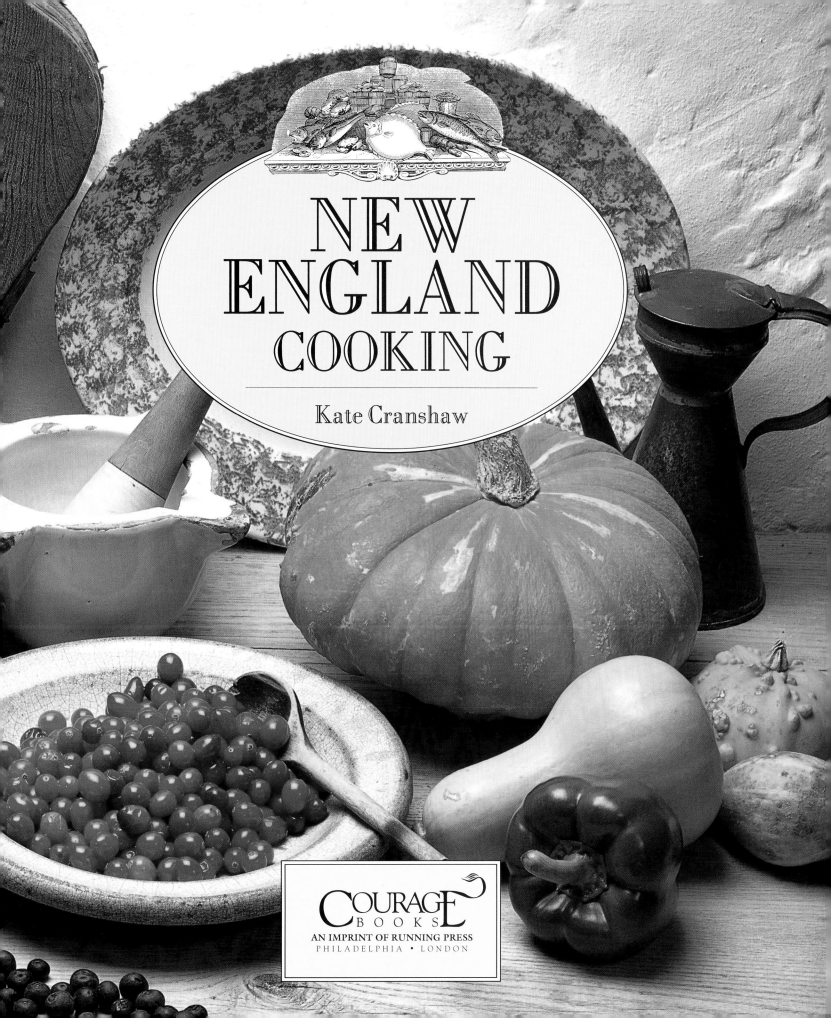

NEW ENGLAND COOKING

Kate Cranshaw

COURAGE BOOKS

AN IMPRINT OF RUNNING PRESS
PHILADELPHIA • LONDON

CLB 4276
9 8 7 6 5 4 3 2 1
Digit on the right indicated the number of this
printing.

Library of Congress Cataloging-in-Publication
Number 94-72602

ISBN 1-56138-563-8

This book was designed and produced by
CLB Publishing, Godalming, Surrey, England.

Editor: Kate Cranshaw
Senior Editor: Jillian Stewart
Introduction: Bill Harris
Designers: Alison Lee and Julie Smith
Picture Researcher: Leora Kahn
Photographers: Neil Sutherland and Peter Barry

Typesetting by Inforum
Printed and bound in Singapore

Published by Courage Books,
an imprint of Running Press Book Publishers
125 South Twenty-second Street
Philadelphia, PA 19103-4399

*First page: an old photograph
of the splendid Faneuil Hall in
Boston. Right: the Jenney Grist
Mill at Plymouth, Massachusetts.*

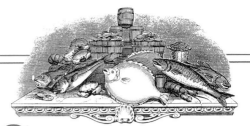

Contents

Introduction

Above: traders unload their wagons ready for a busy day at Faneuil Hall Market in Boston.

Jean Anthelme Brillat-Savarin's 1825 work "The Physiology of Taste" – arguably the most famous book ever written about food – includes a few observations from a three-year sojourn in America, which he said was a moderate success because "... I took care not to seem more intelligent than they, and I was pleased with whatever they did; it was thus that I paid for the hospitality I found among them by a tactfulness which I believe necessary."

Among the places he visited was a farm "five whole ungodly leagues" from Hartford, Connecticut, where he had been invited to join a hunt for wild turkeys. Expecting the worst, as was consistent with his nature, he was delightfully charmed by the farmer's daughters. He was also disarmed by the meal the girls and their mother

Right: Mark Twain House in Hartford, Connecticut.

prepared for him, which included "a handsome piece of corned beef, a stewed goose and a magnificent leg of mutton, then plenty of root vegetables of all kinds." During the hunting expedition the following day, Brillat-Savarin claims to be the only one of the party who bagged a turkey and because of his accomplishment, which he characterized as "historic," he was invited to prepare it for dinner. Although he declined to say exactly how he roasted the bird, he modestly reported that "it was charming to look at, flattering to the sense of smell and delicious to the taste. And as the last morsel of it disappeared, there arose from the whole table the words: 'Very good! Exceedingly good! Oh! Dear Sir, what a glorious bit!'"

The four girls were probably just as happy to get the afternoon off, not to mention not having to deal with leftover turkey. But few farm women in early nineteenth-century Connecticut, or anywhere else in New England, felt the need for the input of a French chef around their kitchen fires. They and their grandmothers had been doing very nicely on their own since the Pilgrim fathers landed on the shores of Cape Cod in 1620.

Although it is one of the most historic meals ever served in New England, almost as little is known of the turkey dinner that marked their first Thanksgiving as of Brillat-Savarin's. If they served turkey at all, it would have been the predominantly dark meat of tough old wild birds that weighed forty pounds or more. They were more often than not infested with ticks and lice in the wild, and had to be skinned before roasting on a spit over an open fire. In order to preserve the juices and save the flavor, they were usually rubbed with clay, an idea that came from the natives, who were not only the guests at the feast for which they provided much of the food, but passed along many such culinary tips that had served them well for generations.

As in other parts of North America, the Native Americans introduced the newcomers to corn, and in New England they grew beans along with it, using the cornstalks to provide support for the vines. It seemed only natural that if they grew together, they ought to be eaten together and the combination of cooked corn and beans is still called by their name for it, succotash. It was undoubtedly part of the bill of fare at the first Thanksgiving, made from dried corn kernels and pea beans seasoned with bear fat, an ingredient as indispensable to the Algonquins as salt is to modern cooks. The newcomers were also introduced to such New England staples as maple sugar, blueberries, pumpkins, and quahogs and other shellfish, which sustained the Pilgrims during their first winter in the New World.

It was the second wave of English immigrants, the Puritans who settled around Boston Bay in 1630, who gave us the enduring gift of Boston baked beans. Because they took the Ten Commandments seriously, Puritan women were not allowed to do any cooking on the Sabbath and Sunday dinner had to be prepared the day before, which made Saturday a very busy day, indeed. To cut down their workload, they put a crock of beans, seasoned with pork and molasses, onions and mustard, on the hearth every Saturday morning and by evening, with no effort required except to add a bit of water every now and then, Saturday's dinner had taken care of itself. Left simmering overnight, it also served as Sunday's breakfast. All that was needed to make a perfect meal was brown bread, served steaming from the same fire. It is still a favorite Saturday night supper all over New England, although not all New Englanders agree on how it should be made. In the mountains of Vermont and New Hampshire, they prefer pinto beans to the pea beans favored by the Bostonians, and they usually substitute maple syrup for the molasses. None of the traditionalists use tomatoes in any form because, of course, their Puritan ancestors regarded the fruit they called "love apples" as poisonous.

A baked bean dinner in modern New England also often includes creamy coleslaw and pickles and plenty of applesauce. The cabbage for the slaw, the cucumbers for the pickles, and the apples for the sauce all have their roots in the Old World and were propagated from seed by the first colonists. When the English first arrived in Massachusetts, the only apples growing wild in New England were crabapples, but they wasted no time planting orchards, both from seeds and from cuttings and even before the Puritans arrived, the spring landscape south of Boston was enhanced by apple blossoms. The idea took hold, and by the beginning of the twentieth century, there were more than 8,000 different varieties growing in America. The apples also gave the colonists the means of making another New England standby, cider, which was served at every meal, but was especially popular at breakfast. The cider we drink today is often homogenized or contains preservatives to retard fermentation, but our colonial ancestors had no such additives and within weeks of its pressing, cider generally turned "hard," or in translation, alcoholic. The longer the winter, the harder the cider got, but in spite of their religious scruples, the Puritans loved their morning eye-openers.

Although the Native Americans showed their new neighbors how to dig for clams along the coast and how to catch spawning shad in tidal rivers, they never felt the need to venture out on the open sea in search of food.

Above: the fishing village of Stonington on Deer Isle, like many others in Maine, has a thriving lobster industry.

But such expeditions were second nature to the English, and from the very beginning they turned their backs on forests full of game to harvest haddock, mackerel, and halibut from the ocean. But it was the codfish that became their most important cash crop. Cod was so abundant in their corner of the Atlantic, it also became New England's most important export and wherever it was sold, whether in Europe or the Carolinas, the returning ships brought other food and spices back home, adding to the quality of life as well as expanding New England's culinary horizons. But not all the cod went abroad. The New Englanders had plenty of uses for it right at home. It could be combined with mashed potatoes and eggs and deep fried as codfish cakes; it could be made into chowder or a boiled dinner or turned into hash for breakfast. And whole codfish stuffed and baked was a New England delicacy usually called "Cape Cod turkey."

But the greatest of all New England delicacies is the lobster, whose home is in the icy waters of the Atlantic off the New England coast from Maine to Rhode`Island. Although they have close relatives living elsewhere, the New England branch of the family is far and away the best of breed. It has a cousin in Northern Europe, which the English also call a lobster, the Germans a *hummer*, and the French *homard*, but although there is very little difference between it and our *hommarus Americanus*, except for the color, even people who think everything about Europe is better than anything America produces can't help remarking that homard makes a second-rate lobster dinner.

Actually, Americans took a long time to discover what a gift nature had given to them. The early colonists found lobsters more a nuisance than a delicacy, and generations of farmers collected them along the New England shore to use for fertilizer. The only people who ate them were the very poor who couldn't afford any other food, and in time, when following the American Dream made some of them rich, they went right on eating lobster and their friends were impressed. By the middle of the nineteenth-century, Maine fishermen discovered a profitable sideline by setting out wooden traps baited with dead fish for hungry lobsters and soon Canadians began harvesting them, too, with almost their entire catch going south to the United States. It became such a huge business that by the middle of this century, environmentalists began calling *hommarus Americanus* an endangered species. Whether they are right or not, the fact is that the catch does seem to be getting smaller every year and the size of the lobsters themselves is getting smaller, too.

Common wisdom has it that bigger lobsters are older and therefore tougher, but the fact is that age and size are not really related. The growth cycle is determined by many factors including water temperature, salinity, and the available food supply. Lobsters often lose claws fighting and, though these can be regenerated, it is at the expense of their own growth; it takes two complete molting cycles to produce a new claw. The lobster's claws, which many people consider the tastiest part, are not identical. The bigger one on the left is designed for crushing or breaking shells and the other is adapted for tearing to pull out the meat from inside. It may seem like an efficient system, but nature played a nasty trick as neither claw can reach the lobster's mouth. Pincers, on its walking legs, have to slide the morsels in the general direction of the mouth, with the result that much of a lobster's intended dinner usually winds up as food for passing fish.

Once State O' Mainers discovered that the lobster itself made a dandy dinner, they also found that the best way to prepare one was to plunge it, still alive, into boiling seawater. Others swear it is much better, not to mention easier to eat, split in two and then drizzled with butter and broiled. Either way, it is invariably served along with melted butter. Eating a lobster is an art in itself that often seems like a lot of work, but it is nothing less than a labor of love. The claws should be twisted off first and then split open with a nutcracker after which the meat inside comes out easily. Next, the tail is pulled from the body and then placed on the plate shell down while the cartilage is cut with a knife and the meat removed and then the same process is repeated for the body. The green "tomally" is the lobster's liver and is quite tasty, and a female lobster also yields pink roe, known to afficionados as "coral." Both are frequently added to to the melted butter, but many lobster-lovers eat those parts first.

Lobsters are also the star of any good New England clambake, which is to the Northeast what a pit barbecue is to the Southwest. The difference is that New Englanders never disagree about how the food should be prepared and what should be served. It is a ritual that has been accepted and revered for generations.

The classic clambake is always held on a beach where a pit about a foot deep has been dug in the sand and then lined with stones. A driftwood fire is allowed to burn for about an hour until the stones are white-hot, then the ashes are scraped away and the stones covered with a thin layer of seaweed. A piece of chicken wire comes next and once it is in place over the hot stones, clams that have been scrubbed in sea water and unshucked ears of corn that have also been dipped in sea water are piled on top along with fresh-killed lobsters. More seaweed goes over the top and a piece of sail canvas is placed on it to keep the steam from escaping. About an hour later, assuming the cooks have moved quickly enough to prevent the rocks from cooling, the feast is ready.

Hard-shelled clams come in three basic sizes, ranging from the smallest littlenecks to medium cherrystones to the big chowder clams New Englanders call quahogs. They are often served on the half-shell, raw or baked or broiled in butter, but getting a raw clam open can be as tricky to the uninitiated as getting the cork out of a champagne bottle without hitting the ceiling. As almost everyone in coastal New England knows, the clam should be thoroughly chilled to relax its muscle and then placed in the palm of the left hand with the hinged end facing the hand's heel. A wide flat knife is inserted between the shells close to the muscle and once a small opening is made, the left hand closes into a fist forcing it in deeper to cut the muscle and a quick twist of the right wrist turns the knife and separates the two shells. It takes a little practice, but very little, and once you've mastered the art, you'll be as popular as a piano player at a cocktail party.

Some clams are more cooperative than others, and another New England favorite is the soft-shell variety

from more northern waters. These oval-shaped mollusks come equipped with a protruding neck called a "siphon," and are usually served steamed or fried. The best part is that steaming opens the clams and the siphon provides a neat little handle to remove it. So-called steamers are usually served in big bowls on tables covered with newspapers, necessary because they can be messy and it is simple to clean up the shells by bundling them up in the paper. They are always accompanied by the broth they were cooked in along with dishes of melted butter flavored with lemon. The morsels, held by the neck, are first dipped in the broth and then in the butter. The neck itself is edible, but chewy, and many choose to discard it.

The biggest clams, the quahogs, are the basis for New England clam chowder, a source of pride and controversy from the northern stretches of Maine to Connecticut's border with New York. It is New York, specifically Manhattan, where the controversy comes from; their clam chowder is usually dismissed by New Englanders as thinly disguised vegetable soup. Up north it is a concoction made with milk and rich cream, potatoes and onions, salt pork and clams. New Yorkers add stewed tomatoes to theirs rather than milk, and if that cuts the cholesterol, in the opinion of just about everybody in Boston, or all America for that matter, the tomatoes also overpower the flavor of the clams.

The tradition of using milk in chowders goes back to colonial times when long lean winters forced New Englanders to find nourishment any way they could. One of the staples of their winter diet was a stew made from potatoes and other root vegetables that survived in cold storage, cooked in milk which added to its vitamin and

Above: an 1873 engraving showing a country woman cooking over an open fire.

mineral content. Another winter favorite was the New England boiled dinner which contained meat that could be preserved to last all winter long. We still call it what they named it, corned beef. It was usually cooked in a big pot of water with plenty of root vegetables added, and then served with horseradish, pickles, and mustard. In many homes in eighteenth-century New England, the same meal was repeated three or four times a week. And on the other days, the leftovers were chopped and fried in salt pork drippings along with chopped beets whose color gave the concoction the name red flannel hash.

The original settlers in Massachusetts found such fare not just adequate, but something to be thankful for, and mealtime was always a blessed event, whether the offering was salted cod, corned beef, or poor man's chowder. No matter what it was, it was always brought to the table in a steaming kettle and ladled into small wooden bowls. Because the Puritans considered the bowls an extravagance, children always shared them or were sometimes forced to eat from depressions hollowed out from the edge of the tabletop itself. They all ate with wooden spoons and although their English cousins had discovered forks through the Italians many years earlier, such affectations were shunned in Boston, and forks weren't accepted in proper homes there until well after 1700. Even then, they were considered a handy utensil for holding meat while it was being cut, but certainly not convenient for eating. It would take another fifty years for knives and forks to become common on New England tables and almost overnight, on the eve of the American revolution, eating with one's fingers became declassé.

Most of the food of the colonials was in the form of soups and stews and spoons served very nicely to eat it, with a little help from chunks of bread that were used to soak up gravy and leftover fat. If a piece of meat needed to be cut down to bite size, nearly everybody carried their own knives to do the job. The American custom of eating with one's left hand under the table and the knife placed on the table, rather than following the two-fisted European style of keeping the knife in one hand and the fork in the other, dates back to these personal knives, which could also double as weapons. It was considered polite to leave the blade in plain sight slightly out of reach so that no one would mistake the owner's intention.

It is hard to imagine anyone of Puritan hertitage ever threatening anyone, but by the 1700s there were strangers in their midst, including the Portuguese, many of whom traced their own American roots back to fishermen who arrived ahead of the English. As each new ethnic group arrived, they brought changes to New England's cuisine. The Irish, for instance, altered the traditional boiled dinner by substituting cabbage for the parsnips, turnips, and carrots. And what would St. Patrick's Day be to a modern Bostonian without a dinner of corned beef and cabbage?

The popular image of the New England Puritans is of long-suffering folks whose daily lives revolved around hard work and Bible study. But although they took their religion seriously, all of them believed that a day without beer, in addition to their beloved hard cider, was like a day without sunshine. Among the reasons they claim to have landed on Cape Cod rather than in Virginia, which was their intended destination, the Pilgrims said they could go no further because their beer supply was running low. And among the grains and seeds they had brought with them for planting, the most important was barley, which they intended to convert to malt for making beer, the very staff of life as far as they were concerned. A generation or two later, Rhode Island became the richest of the New England colonies because of its bustling rum distilleries. And although most of it was exported, a good deal of it stayed right at home. It was consumed in every New England home and became the main attraction at springtime frolics known as fish fries. Even before the ice began to melt in the rivers, shad by the thousands swam in from the sea to spawn and New Englanders, a little tired of boiled dinners and red flannel hash by that point, rushed to the riverbanks where the fish were easily caught and fried them over open fires right on the spot. Such work can make a person thirsty, and the thirst-quencher of choice was rum punch. But don't let the word "punch" fool you. It consisted of a mug of rum diluted a bit with pieces of ice from the river, quite possibly America's first example of a drink "on the rocks." Yes, invented by Puritans.

None of that is to suggest that our ancestors were a bunch of drunken louts. Far from it, they did the best they could with what they had, and as you are about to discover, left a wonderful historical and culinary legacy for us to enjoy.

CHAPTER ONE

Soups and Appetizers

*Above: Sandwich, first settled by Pilgrims in 1637,
is the oldest town on Cape Cod.*

*Traditional soups and appetizers from New England
sail a flagship for the rest of the cuisine, for they make
wonderful use of some of the best loved and tastiest of the
local ingredients: clams and seafood, apples, pumpkin,
and squashes. The apples were, of course, one of the
most important ingredients brought into the country by the
immigrants from the Old World, who also learned
a lot about local produce from the Native Americans, who
were the first to show them how to find, cook, and enjoy
the wonderful range of seafoods available in
New England waters.*

Right: Cream of Pumpkin Soup.

Clam Chowder

The chowder owes its name to the French fishermen who would celebrate the safe return of the fleet by cooking fish soup on the docks in huge kettles or chaudières.

2 pounds clams (or 1 pound shelled or canned clams)
All-purpose flour
3 oz rindless bacon, diced
2 medium onions, finely diced
1 Tbsp all-purpose flour
6 medium potatoes, peeled and cubed
Salt and pepper
4 cups milk
1 cup light cream
Chopped fresh parsley (optional)

Scrub the clams well and place them in a basin of cold water with a handful of flour to soak for 30 minutes. Drain the clams and place them in a deep saucepan with about ½ cup cold water. Cover and bring to a boil, stirring occasionally until all the shells open. Discard any that do not open. Strain the clam liquid and reserve it and set the clams aside to cool.

Place the diced bacon in a large, deep saucepan and cook slowly until the fat is rendered. Turn up the heat and brown the bacon. Remove it to a paper towel to drain. Add the onions to the bacon fat in the pan and cook slowly to soften. Stir in the flour and add the potatoes, salt, pepper, milk, and reserved clam juice. Cover, bring to a boil and cook for about 10 minutes, or until the potatoes are nearly tender. Remove the clams from their shells and chop them if large. Add to the soup along with the cream and diced bacon. Cook for a further 10 minutes, or until the potatoes and clams are tender. Add the chopped parsley, if desired, and serve immediately. Serves 6-8.

Above left: an engraving of John Adams, the second president of the United States (1797-1801). Adams was born in 1735 in Braintree, Massachusetts.

14

Country Pâté

In traditional farming communities nothing is left to waste, and this wonderful coarse-textured pâté shows just how tasty a dish can be made from meat that is sometimes overlooked.

1 pig's head (to yield 1½ pounds cooked meat, cleaned)
2 medium onions
1 carrot
1¼ pounds pork liver
2½ pounds fresh pork butt
Salt and white pepper
2 cloves garlic
2 Tbsps butter

Purchase a cleaned pig's head from a butcher. Rinse it thoroughly and place in a large pot with enough water to cover. Add 1 of the onions and the carrot, peeled and chopped. Simmer for at least 2 hours or until the meat is falling from the bones. Remove the meat from the pot and allow to cool. Remove the meat from the bone and weigh out the 1½ pounds needed. Meanwhile, dice the liver and pork butt. Season with salt and pepper and refrigerate for 12 hours.
Preheat the oven to 300° F. Dice the remaining onion and garlic cloves and sauté in the butter. Combine with all the other prepared ingredients and run the mixture through a grinding machine on medium grinding plate.
Place the ground mixture in a terrine with a tightly fitting cover. Bake in the oven, covered, for about 2½ hours. Leave to cool then refrigerate for 48 hours before serving. Serves 6.

Autumn Bisque

Butternut squash and apples are at their best in the fall. They were both staple foods grown by the settlers for their keeping qualities. They complement one another well and taste delicious in a smooth, creamy soup.

1 1-pound butternut squash, unpeeled, halved, and seeded
2 green apples, peeled, cored, and chopped
1 medium onion, chopped
Pinch of rosemary and marjoram
1 quart chicken stock
2 slices white bread, trimmed and cubed
1½ tsps salt
¼ tsp pepper
2 egg yolks
¼ cup heavy cream

Combine the squash, apples, onion, herbs, stock, bread cubes, salt, and pepper in a heavy saucepan. Bring to a boil and simmer, uncovered, for 30-45 minutes. Take out the squash with a draining spoon and scoop out the flesh, discarding the skins. Return the pulp to the soup. Purée the soup in a blender or food processor until smooth and return to the rinsed out saucepan. In a small bowl, beat the egg yolks and cream together. Beat in a little of the hot soup and then stir back into the saucepan with the rest of the soup. Cook gently, stirring constantly, until thickened. Do not allow the soup to boil or the eggs will curdle. Serve immediately. Serves 4-6.

Right: the picturesque village of Peru, typical of many in Vermont, is dotted with the pretty white farmhouses that are characteristic of New England.

Cape Cod Mussels

When seafood is as good as that from Cape Cod, even the simplest preparations stand out.

4½ pounds live mussels
Flour or cornmeal
1 cup dry white wine
1 large onion, finely chopped
2-4 cloves garlic, finely chopped
Salt and coarsely ground black pepper
2 bay leaves
1 cup butter, melted
Juice of 1 lemon

Scrub the mussels well and remove any barnacles and beards (seaweed strands). Use a stiff brush to scrub the shells, and discard any mussels with broken shells or those that do not close when tapped. Place the mussels in a basin full of cold water with a handful of flour or cornmeal and leave to soak for 30 minutes.

Drain the mussels and place them in a large, deep saucepan with the wine, onion, garlic, salt and pepper, and bay leaves. Cover the pan and bring to a boil. Stir the mussels occasionally while they are cooking to help them cook evenly. Cook about 5-8 minutes, or until the shells open. Discard any mussels that do not open. Spoon the mussels into individual serving bowls and strain the cooking liquid. Pour the liquid into 4 small bowls and serve with the mussels and a bowl of the melted butter mixed with the lemon juice for each person. Dip the mussels into the broth and the melted butter to eat. Use a mussel shell to scoop out each mussel, or eat with small forks or spoons. Serves 4.

Above left: a period photograph of the Newburyport fish market, Massachusetts. Many of the old commercial buildings of this previously important port have been carefully restored to their former glory.

Green Pea Soup

Stuffed Quahogs

Quahogs are hard-shell clams that are used for chowder when large, and eaten on the half shell when smaller. To facilitate opening, place well-scrubbed clams in a pan in a moderate oven and heat until they open. Use a strong knife to pry off the top shells.

3 Tbsps butter
1 onion, chopped
1 green and 1 red bell pepper, chopped
1 clove garlic, minced
¼ tsp oregano
8 quahogs, shelled, poached for 3 minutes and chopped
Fresh bread crumbs
4 tsps grated Romano or Parmesan cheese
Lemon wedges and hot pepper sauce to serve

Dried peas have been a staple food in America since the first settlers set foot on dry land. Almost every country in the Western world has a recipe for pea soup and the addition of a ham bone adds extra flavor.

1 package split green peas (no soaking required)
1 Tbsp grated onion
1 celery stalk, thinly sliced
1 carrot, thinly sliced
1 ham bone with some meat attached
Chopped fresh parsley

Crackers to serve

Pick over the split peas and add them to a large pot along with all the other ingredients. Cover with water and cook for 30-40 minutes, adding more water if needed. Remove the bone from the soup, take off the meat and chop it finely. Return the meat to the soup, sprinkle with parsley and serve with crackers. Serves 6-8.

Preheat the oven to 375°F. Heat the butter in a pan and sauté the onion and peppers until glassy, add the garlic and oregano; cook for another 1-2 minutes over a low heat. Stir in the chopped clams with an equal amount of fresh bread crumbs, and the cheese. Moisten with additional melted butter and/ or clam juice. Stuff into each clam shell half and bake in the oven for about 10 minutes until hot and slightly browned. Serve with lemon wedges and hot pepper sauce. Serves 4.

Above left: in the days before mechanization, preparing food by hand could often be a long and laborious process. Right: the Pliny Freeman Farm in Massachusetts demonstrates facets of nineteenth-century life.

Cream of Pumpkin Soup

Pumpkins have an honored place in American culinary history and show up in many different preparations. This is a particular New Hampshire favorite.

1 large pumpkin, about 4-5 pounds in weight
¼ cup butter or margarine
1 large onion, sliced
1 cup heavy cream
Pinch of salt, white pepper, and nutmeg
Chopped fresh chives to garnish (optional)

Wash the pumpkin well on the outside and cut through horizontally, about 2 inches down from the stem end. Carefully cut most of the pulp off the top and reserve the "lid" for later use. Remove the seeds from the inside and discard them. Using a small, sharp knife, carefully remove all but ½ inch of the pulp from inside the pumpkin. Work slowly and carefully to avoid piercing the outer skin of the pumpkin. Chop all the pulp from the top and the inside of the pumpkin and set it aside. Melt the butter or margarine in a large saucepan and add the onion. Cook slowly until the onion is tender but not brown. Add the pumpkin flesh and about 4 cups of cold water. Bring to a boil and then allow to simmer gently, covered, for about 20 minutes.

Purée the mixture in a food processor or blender in several small batches. Return the soup to the pot and add the cream, salt, pepper, and nutmeg to taste. Reheat the soup and pour it into the reserved pumpkin shell. Garnish the top of the soup with chopped chives, if desired, before serving. Serves 6-8.

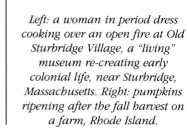

Left: a woman in period dress cooking over an open fire at Old Sturbridge Village, a "living" museum re-creating early colonial life, near Sturbridge, Massachusetts. Right: pumpkins ripening after the fall harvest on a farm, Rhode Island.

CHAPTER TWO

Fish and Seafood

Above: an atmospheric old photograph of a chef busy at work in the galley of a yacht.

66Once the tide is out, the table is set," is an old Native American saying, and certainly the new settlers soon learned how prolific was the harvest of seafood – clams and lobsters in particular – along the coast. The English settlers, of course, were natural sailors, and began to fish farther out to sea and bring back such delicacies as sea trout to supplement the river fish that they caught after the spring thaw. In Maine and Rhode Island, seafood is the major specialty on the menu, and the freshness and flavor of their dishes is unmistakable.

Right: Baked Sea Trout in Parchment.

Boatman's Stew

There are many different influences in some of the cooking of New England. This recipe is very similar to Portuguese Fish Stew, while the toasted bread in the bottom of the bowl reveals a French input as well.

6 Tbsps olive oil
2 large onions, sliced
1 red bell pepper, sliced
¼ pound mushrooms, sliced
1 pound canned tomatoes
Pinch of dried thyme
Pinch of salt and pepper
1½ cups water
2 pounds whitefish fillets, skinned
½ cup white wine
2 Tbsps chopped fresh parsley
Toasted French bread to serve

Heat the oil in a large saucepan and add the onions. Cook until beginning to look transluscent. Add the pepper and cook until the vegetables are softened. Add the mushrooms and the tomatoes and bring the mixture to a boil. Add the thyme, salt, pepper, and water and simmer for about 30 minutes.
Add the fish and wine and cook until the fish flakes easily, about 15 minutes. Stir in the parsley. To serve, place a piece of toasted French bread in the bottom of the soup bowl and spoon over the fish stew. Serves 4-6.

Above left: Mystic Seaport, Connecticut, occupies the site of a once-thriving shipyard. The "living" museum consists of over 60 reconstructed period buildings, as well as preserved and replica sailing vessels. Craftspeople practice traditional maritime crafts to re-create the atmosphere of a nineteenth-century seaport.

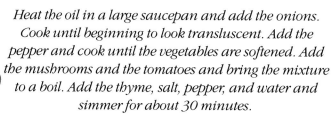

Baked Sea Trout in Parchment

This simple dish from Rhode Island demonstrates the French influence on the local cooking. Fish is baked en papillote *or in paper parcels, which preserves all its wonderful flavor and juices. The parcels are opened at the table for full effect.*

1-1¼ pounds sea trout fillet
2 sheets baking paper or foil
4 slices Spanish onion
4 slices fresh tomato
4 rings green bell pepper
4 mussels, cleaned and debearded
4 sprigs of fresh thyme and sage
2 white peppercorns, crushed
Melted butter
White wine

Preheat the oven to 350°F. Divide the fish into two equal portions and place skinned side down on two sheets of baking paper. Garnish the fish with onion slices, tomato slices, and then pepper rings. Place the mussels on top and then the herbs and pepper. Drizzle a little melted butter and wine on the fish and then seal the paper parcels, twisting the ends well. Coat the outsides with additional melted butter and bake in the oven for about 20 minutes. Serves 2.

Above right: this engraving depicts the mass of trade ships that the Dutch West India Company sent to New England after the early part of the seventeenth century.

Right: West Quoddy Light, built in 1858, marks the easternmost point of the United States. It is one of an essential chain of lighthouses that guide sailors safely round the many rocky outcrops along the Maine coastline.

Boston Scrod

The curved peninsula of Cape Cod was named by early explorers because of its impressive schools of codfish. Even now, cod dishes are extremely popular in Massachusetts.

4 even-sized scrod fillets
Salt and pepper
⅓ cup butter, melted
¾ cup dry bread crumbs
1 tsp dry mustard
1 tsp onion salt
Dash of Worcestershire sauce
Dash of Tabasco sauce
2 Tbsps lemon juice
1 Tbsp finely chopped fresh parsley

Season the fish fillets with salt and pepper and place them on a broiler tray. Brush with butter and broil for about 5 minutes. Combine the remaining butter with bread crumbs, mustard, onion salt, Worcestershire sauce, Tabasco, lemon juice, and parsley. Spoon the mixture carefully on top of each fish fillet, covering it completely. Press down lightly to pack the crumbs into place. Broil for another 5-7 minutes, or until the top is lightly browned and the fish flakes easily. Serves 4.

Above: Acorn Street, with its beautiful red-brick houses, is part of the splendidly preserved Beacon Hill district in Boston.

Above left: this charming period photograph depicts a family riverside picnic at the turn of the century.

North Atlantic Salmon Amandine

Traditionally, salmon was served in New England to celebrate the Fourth of July. This recipe again shows the French influence common in the region.

5-6 pound whole salmon, cleaned

COURT BOUILLON
4 cups water
3 celery stalks, diced
1 onion quartered and stuck with whole cloves

STUFFING
6 cups crushed Ritz crackers
5 Tbsps butter, melted
¾ cup cream sherry
2 tsps salt
2 tsps Worcestershire sauce
2 drops Tabasco sauce
1½ pounds Maine crab meat

GARNISH
1 pound blanched, sliced almonds
1 egg white

Cut the underside of the salmon from the end of the slit from where it was cleaned, up to the tip of the tail. Set the fish belly-side down and spread out the cut underside.

Press down along the backbone of the fish, pushing the spine downwards. Turn the fish over and pull the backbone away using a sharp knife, then cut it out at the base of the head and tail using a pair of scissors. Preheat the oven to 350° F. Combine the fish bones with the court bouillon ingredients in a saucepan or fish steamer. Bring to a boil and simmer for 20 minutes, then allow to cool while preparing the stuffing. Combine all the stuffing ingredients and mix well. Spoon the stuffing into the cavity of the salmon. Brush the fish with melted butter and place in the top of the fish steamer or into a roasting pan. If using a roasting pan, carefully pour the cooled court bouillon over the fish. Cover with foil and steam in the oven for about 50 minutes. Remove the fish from the steamer or roasting pan and peel the skin from one side of the fish from the head to the tail, leaving the head and tail intact. Garnish the side of the fish with the almonds, using egg white to hold them in place, to give the fish a scale effect. Brown under a preheated broiler until golden. Serves 8.

Above left: the pretty fishing village of Port Clyde, Maine. Right: Dolley Madison, wife of President Madison, saving the Declaration of Independence in 1814 after the White House was set on fire by British troops during "Mr. Madison's War."

Boiled Maine Lobster

With today's lobster prices, it's hard to imagine that American colonists considered this delectable seafood humble and ordinary.

Maine Steamed Clams

Maine clams are soft-shell clams and are delicious steamed, fried, or in chowders. As part of a Maine Shore Dinner, they are often called steamers and are served in great piles alongside lobster and corn on the cob.

PER PERSON
7-8 medium sized soft-shell clams (steamers), scrubbed
¼ cup water
½-1 cup butter, melted

Water
Salt or seaweed
4 1-pound live lobsters
Lemon wedges
Fresh parsley sprigs to garnish
1 cup butter, melted

Fill a large stock pot full of water and add salt or a piece of seaweed. Bring the water to a boil and then turn off the heat. Place the live lobsters into the pot, keeping your hand well away from the claws. Lower them in claws first. Bring the water slowly back to a boil and cook the lobsters for about 15 minutes, or until they turn bright red. Remove them from the water and drain briefly on paper towels. Place on a plate and garnish the plate with lemon wedges and parsley sprigs. Serve with individual dishes of melted butter for dipping. Serves 4.

Place the clams in a medium-sized kettle with the water. Cover and cook on medium heat until the clam juice (referred to in Maine as clam broth) boils up through the clams and all the clams are opened. Discard any that do not open. Serve them hot with melted butter and the clam broth. To eat, remove the tissue from the neck, dip the clam in the broth and then into the butter. Serves 1.

Above left: the superbly preserved kitchen of Fort Western in Augusta, Maine. The building, a fine example of colonial architecture, dates from 1754 and is now a museum.

Maine Lobster Stew

This is another and probably the most luxurious of the famous shellfish soup-stews from the East Coast. The dill pickles may seem an unusual choice as an accompaniment, but their piquancy is a perfect foil for the velvety richness of the stew.

4 quarts whole milk
¼ cup heavy cream
¼ cup melted butter
1½ tsps paprika
3¼ pounds Maine lobster meat
Pinch of salt
Oyster crackers, dill pickles, and hot rolls to serve

Heat the milk and heavy cream in a double boiler. Do not allow to boil. In a heavy skillet (preferably cast iron), slowly heat the melted butter and paprika, mixing them together to create a red butter sauce. Add the cold Maine lobster and heat slowly, turning the meat until warm, but do not over-heat. Add the warmed lobster meat to the hot milk and heat gently for at least 1 hour. Add a pinch of salt if necessary. For best results, remove the lobster stew from the heat and refrigerate overnight. Reheat the next day. Serve with oyster crackers, dill pickles, and hot rolls. Serves 8-10.

Butter Fish

These light, tasty fish, also known as dollarfish, are one of New England's principal fish. They are best cooked simply, as this recipe shows you, to preserve their delicate flavor.

4-8 butter fish, gutted
2-4 Tbsps butter
Lemon slices

Place 1-2 fish per person on a hot griddle and brush with butter. Cook over a low heat for about 3 minutes. The fish may not need to be turned. Garnish each fish with half a thin slice of lemon. Serve as a side dish at any meal. Serves 4.

Above left: a Boston fisherman selling his wares on the wharf. Right: Mayflower II, a replica of the ship that brought the Pilgrim Fathers to America in 1620, is moored at Plymouth, Massachusetts.

CHAPTER THREE

Meat, Poultry, and Game

Above: the basic kitchen of the Jethro Coffin House in the town of Nantucket, Massachusetts, depicts the simple lifestyle of early New England settlers. The house, built in 1686, is believed to be the oldest house on Nantucket island.

*W*ith such a variety of landscapes in the region, almost every type of livestock and game is available to grace the table. From the extensive forests and grasslands of New Hampshire come wild duck and game, cattle from the lush grasslands of Vermont, and chickens from the farms of Massachusetts. The Shaker traditions of simple, hearty presentation influence some of the dishes, but there are also touches of French, Italian, and genuine American innovation among the range of delicious dishes.

Right: Venison Stew.

Yankee Pot Roast

This classic American recipe, traditionally cooked in an iron pot or Dutch oven, has its roots in French and German cuisine, notably the sauerbraten *brought over by the Amish.*

3 pounds beef roast (rump, chuck, round, or top end)
Flour seasoned with salt and pepper
2 Tbsps butter or margarine
1 onion stuck with 2 cloves
1 bay leaf
2 tsps fresh thyme or 1 tsp dried thyme
1 cup beef stock
4 carrots
12 small onions, peeled
4 small turnips, peeled and left whole
2 potatoes, cut into even-sized pieces
2 Tbsps butter or margarine
2 Tbsps all-purpose flour

Dredge the beef with the seasoned flour, patting off the excess. Melt the butter in a large, heavy-based casserole or saucepan and, when foaming, brown the meat on all sides, turning it with wooden spoons or a spatula. When well browned, add the onion stuck with the cloves, the bay leaf, and thyme and pour on the stock. Cover the pan, reduce the heat and simmer on top of the stove or cook in a preheated 300° F oven. Cook slowly for about 2 hours, adding more liquid, either stock or water, as necessary.

Test the meat and, if beginning to feel tender, add the vegetables. Cover and continue to cook until the meat is completely tender and the vegetables are cooked through. Remove the meat and vegetables from the casserole or pan and place them on a warm serving platter. Skim the excess fat from the top of the sauce and bring it back to a boil. Mix the butter and flour (beurre manié) to a smooth paste. Add about 1 tsp of the mixture to the hot sauce and whisk thoroughly. Continue adding the mixture until the sauce is of the desired thickness. Carve the meat and spoon over some of the sauce. Serve the rest of the sauce separately. Serves 6-8.

Above: a Cape Neddick family making butter in 1892. "Churning day" would have been a regular occurance, for many families prepared as much of their food as possible.

40

New England Boiled Dinner

The corning process for preserving beef was a useful one in early America and dates back to Anglo-Saxon Britain, where the dish originates. Beef and salt were layered in a barrel then soaked in a mixture of salt peter, water, molasses, and spices for a couple of weeks. The word "corned" comes from that time, when the size of the salt grains used were the size of wheat kernels – or corn as it was known to them.

3 pound corned beef brisket
1 bay leaf
1 tsp mustard seed
3 allspice berries
3 cloves
1 tsp dill seed
6 black peppercorns
2 potatoes, cut into even-sized pieces
4 small onions
Salt
4 large carrots
4 small or 2 large parsnips, cut into even-sized pieces
1 large or 2 small rutabagas, cut into even-sized pieces
1 medium-sized green cabbage, cored and quartered

Place the corned beef in a large saucepan with enough water to cover and add the bay leaf and spices. Simmer for about 2 hours, skimming any foam from the surface as the meat cooks.
Add the potatoes and onions and cook for about 15 minutes. Taste and add salt if necessary. Add the carrots, parsnips, and rutabagas and cook for another 15 minutes. Add the cabbage and cook another 15 minutes.
Remove the meat from the casserole and slice it thinly. Arrange on a warm serving platter and remove the vegetables from the broth with a draining spoon, placing them around the meat. Serve immediately with horseradish sauce or mustard. Serves 4.

Rhode Island Leg of Lamb

This is a delicious way to roast lamb in a reflector oven. If you do not have this type of oven, preheat your oven to 325° F and roast until the meat is tender and slightly pink in the center.

5-6 pound leg of lamb
4 cloves garlic, halved or quartered depending upon size
Fresh or dried rosemary, crushed

Push a sharp knife into the meat at 5-inch intervals and insert slivers of garlic into the cuts. Rub with rosemary. Pierce the leg with a skewer and place it in the oven. Cook in front of a slow heat at a distance of approximately 18 inches. Turn every 15 minutes for about 1½ hours while basting in its own juices. When the meat looks done, cut a small, deep slice to check the color. Serves 6-8.

Steak over an Open Fire

There is no better way to cook a steak than over an open fire, but a barbecue will do almost as well!

Sea salt, coarsely ground
4 6-8 oz chuck steaks, cut 1-inch thick
12-16 large mushroom caps
2 large onions, thickly sliced

Rub the sea salt on both sides of the meat. Place the mushroom caps and onions on an oiled skillet over a medium heat. The steaks should take only 10-12 minutes to cook, so add them when the vegetables are half cooked. If cooking on a stove cook the steaks for 7-15 minutes depending on taste. Turn the steaks only once while cooking and serve with the mushrooms and onions. Serves 4.

Red Flannel Hash

Vermont Cob-Smoked Ham

Not all hams are the same. Cob smoking gives the Vermont ham a unique and very pleasant taste. Some Vermonters like to baste the ham with fresh apple cider during the last 30 minutes of cooking. Plan to serve three people with each pound of ham.

1 Vermont cob-smoked ham
Fresh apple cider (optional)

Preheat the oven to 300° F. Place the Vermont ham in a large roasting pan and insert a meat thermometer into the thickest part, avoiding the bone. Bake the ham, uncovered, for 12 minutes per pound. When done, the ham should have an internal temperature of 120° F. Serves 3 per pound.

The name of this dish originated when red beets were chopped into the corned beef hash along with whatever leftover vegetables were available.

1 pound cold corned beef
3-4 cold boiled potatoes, roughly chopped
1 medium onion, finely chopped
Salt, pepper, and nutmeg
1-2 cooked beets, peeled and diced
2 Tbsps butter or bacon fat

Cut the meat into small pieces. If using a food processor be careful not to overwork. Combine with all the remaining ingredients except the butter or bacon fat. Melt the butter or fat in a skillet and, when foaming place in the mixture. Spread it out evenly in the pan. Cook over a low heat, pressing the mixture down continuously with a wooden spoon or spatula. Cook for about 15-20 minutes. When a crust forms on the bottom, turn over and brown the other side. Cut into wedges and remove from the skillet to serve. Serves 4.

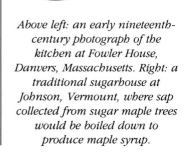

Above left: an early nineteenth-century photograph of the kitchen at Fowler House, Danvers, Massachusetts. Right: a traditional sugarhouse at Johnson, Vermount, where sap collected from sugar maple trees would be boiled down to produce maple syrup.

44

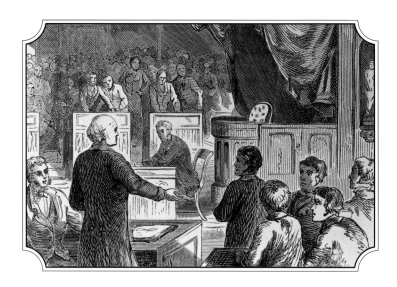

Chicken Pot Pie

There are many versions of this hearty dish from the country farmhouse kitchens. Everyone has their favorite version – some prefer not to include vegetables and others like to use buttermilk in the biscuit topping.

4 chicken joints (2 breasts and 2 legs)
5 cups water
1 bay leaf
2 sprigs of thyme
1 sprig of rosemary
1 sprig fresh tarragon or ¼ tsp dry tarragon
4 whole peppercorns
1 allspice berry
4 Tbsps white wine
2 carrots, diced
24 pearl onions, peeled
6 Tbsps corn kernels
½ cup heavy cream
Salt

BISCUIT TOPPING
3½ cups all-purpose flour
1½ Tbsps baking powder
Pinch of salt
5 Tbsps butter or margarine
1½ cups milk
1 egg, beaten with a pinch of salt

Place the chicken in a deep saucepan with the water, herbs, spices, and wine. Cover and bring to a boil. Reduce the heat and allow to simmer for 20-30 minutes, or until the chicken is tender. Remove the chicken from the pot and allow to cool. Skim and discard the fat from the surface of the stock. Skin the chicken and remove the meat from the bones.

Continue to simmer the stock until reduced by about half. Strain the stock and add the carrots and onions. Cook until tender and add the corn. Stir in the cream and add the chicken. Pour into a casserole or into individual baking dishes. Preheat the oven to 375° F.

To prepare the topping, sift the dry ingredients into a bowl or place them in a food processor and process once or twice to sift. Rub in the butter or margarine until the mixture resembles small peas. Stir in enough of the milk until the mixture comes together. Turn out onto a floured surface and knead lightly. Roll out thickly with a floured rolling pin and cut with a pastry cutter. Brush the surface of each biscuit with the egg. Place the biscuits on top of the chicken mixture and bake in the oven for 10-15 minutes. Serve immediately. Serves 6.

Above left: this engraving shows John Quincy Adams, son of John Adams, speaking in the House of Representatives.

New England Roast Turkey

The Thanksgiving celebration would not be the same without a turkey on the table. Native Americans first domesticated the bird and introduced the early settlers to it.

1 fresh turkey weighing about 20 pounds
⅓ cup butter

SAUSAGE STUFFING
4 Tbsps oil
4 oz sausage meat
3 celery stalks, diced
2 onions, diced
1 cup chopped walnuts or pecans
1 cup raisins
¼ tsp dried thyme
¼ tsp dried sage
2 Tbsps chopped fresh parsley
1 pound day-old bread, cut into small cubes
1 cup chicken stock
Salt and pepper

Pull out any pin feathers on the turkey with tweezers and remove the fat which is just inside the cavity of the bird. Preheat the oven to 325°F.
To prepare the stuffing, heat the oil in a skillet and cook the sausage meat, breaking it up with a fork as it cooks.

Add the celery, onions, nuts, and raisins and cook for about 5 minutes, stirring constantly. Drain away the fat and add the herbs, cubes of bread, and stock and mix well. Season to taste. Stuff the cavity of the bird using your hands or a long-handled spoon. Save some stuffing to tuck under the neck flap to plump it. Sew the cavity of the bird closed, or use skewers to secure it. Tie the legs together but do not cross them over. Tuck the neck skin under the wing tips and, if desired, use a trussing needle and fine string to secure them.
Place the turkey on a rack, breast side up, in a roasting pan. Soften the butter and spread some over the breast and the legs. Place the turkey in the oven and cover loosely with foil. Roast for about 2 hours, basting often. Remove the foil and continue roasting for another 2-2½ hours, or until the internal temperature in the thickest part of the thigh registers 350°F on a meat thermometer. Alternatively, pierce the thigh with a skewer – if the juices run clear then the turkey is done. Allow to rest for about 15-20 minutes before carving. Make gravy with the pan juices, if desired, and serve. Serves 10-12.

Above left: the Job-Macy House in Nantucket, Massachusetts, is one of the well-preserved buildings in this historic town.

Poached Chicken with Cream Sauce

The advantage of simply cooked dishes to the early farmers was that they created a delicious dish with the minimum of effort. Today we prefer more ornate dishes and with a bit of garnishing, this dish looks good enough for special occasions.

4¹⁄₂ pound whole roasting chicken
8-10 celery stalks, cut into 3-inch lengths and tops reserved
4 oz bacon, thickly sliced
2 cloves garlic, minced
1 large onion, stuck with 4 cloves
1 bay leaf
1 sprig of fresh thyme
Salt and pepper
Water to cover
¹⁄₃ cup butter or margarine
6 Tbsps all-purpose flour
1 cup heavy cream

Remove the fat from just inside the cavity of the chicken and pull out any pin feathers with tweezers. Tie the chicken legs together and tuck the wing tips under to hold the neck flap. Place the chicken in a large casserole or stock pot. Chop the celery tops and add to the pot. Place the bacon over the chicken and add the garlic, onion with the cloves, bay leaf, thyme, salt, pepper, and water to cover. Bring to a boil, reduce the heat and simmer gently, covered, for 50 minutes or until the chicken is just tender.

Add the celery and simmer for another 20 minutes, or until the celery is just tender. Remove the chicken to a serving plate and keep warm. Strain the stock and reserve the bacon and celery pieces. Skim off any fat from the top of the stock and add enough water to make up to 2 cups, if necessary.

Melt 1 Tbsp of the butter or margarine in the casserole and sauté the bacon until just crisp. Drain on paper towels and crumble roughly. Melt the rest of the butter in the casserole and, when foaming, take off the heat. Stir in the flour and gradually add the chicken stock. Add the cream and bring to a boil, stirring constantly. Simmer until the mixture is thickened.

Untie the chicken legs and trim the leg ends. If desired, remove the skin from the chicken and coat with the sauce. Garnish with the bacon and the reserved celery pieces. Serves 4.

Above left: mid-lesson at the Boston Cooking School, 1880.

Venison Stew

Vermont has more deer per square mile than any other state, so hunting is popular and recipes for venison are abundant. In the nineteenth century, many French Canadians from Quebec settled in Vermont and their culinary influence is evident in dishes like this, reminiscent of French country stews.

1 quart good quality red wine
¼ cup red wine vinegar
1 bay leaf
2 sprigs of fresh thyme
6 juniper berries
1 medium carrot, cut into ¼-inch cubes
1 medium onion, cut into ¼-inch cubes
2 celery stalks, cut into ¼-inch cubes
4 cloves garlic, minced
6 pounds boneless venison shoulder, cubed
½ cup vegetable oil
½ cup all-purpose flour
Pinch of salt and pepper
1 pound slab bacon, cut in ½-inch pieces
1 pound mushrooms, quartered
Chestnut purée to serve

Combine the wine, vinegar, bay leaf, thyme, juniper, carrot, onion, celery, and garlic in a large bowl. Add the cubed venison and marinate for 24 hours.
Remove the meat and vegetables from the marinade and place in separate bowls. Reserve the marinade.
Heat the oil in a heavy skillet and brown the venison on all sides over high heat. Remove the venison from the skillet to a large pot, repeat the browning process with the vegetables, and add to the venison. Sprinkle the flour over the combined meat and vegetables, stir and add the reserved marinade. Add salt and pepper to taste. Simmer for about 1 hour, remove the vegetables after that time and reserve them. Continue cooking the meat for another 30 minutes or until tender. Meanwhile, blanch the bacon for 3 minutes in boiling water. Drain and sauté in the same skillet used for the venison. Add the bacon to the stew when the venison is tender. Sauté the mushrooms and add to the stew. Cook until all the ingredients are hot and serve immediately. A chestnut purée makes a nice accompaniment. Serves 10-12.

Shaker-Style Chicken

The Shakers were a religious community that flourished in the late eighteenth and early nineteenth centuries in the United States. They were dedicated to productive labor and to a life of perfection – which is mirrored in their style of cooking.

4 skinned and boned chicken breasts
Flour for dusting
2 Tbsps butter
1 apple, peeled, cored, and diced
½ cup apple cider vinegar
2 Tbsps clear honey
½ cup apple cider
¾ cup heavy cream
3 Tbsps chopped fresh parsley

Preheat the oven to 350° F. Salt and pepper the chicken and dust lightly with flour. Heat the butter in an ovenproof pan and brown the breasts skin side down first. Turn over and brown the other side, then place in a roasting pan. Bake in the oven for about 20 minutes, or until cooked through but not dry. Remove the chicken to a hot platter and cover with foil to keep warm. Pour off almost all the fat from the pan and sauté the diced apple until golden then drain on paper towels. Pour off any remaining liquid from the pan and add the vinegar and honey. Reduce over a medium heat until the liquid is almost a glaze, being careful not to let it boil over. Take the pan off the heat and add the apple cider slowly, stirring in gradually. Return the pan to medium heat and continue cooking to reduce by about ¾. Be careful not to let the liquid burn. Pour in the cream and cook over high heat to reduce slightly. Serve the chicken with the sauce and sprinkle with the apple and parsley. Serves 4.

Right: demonstrations of nineteenth-century milling techniques can be seen at the Stony Brook Mill in Brewster, Cape Cod.

Brace of Duck in Pears and Grand Marnier

With New Hampshire's abundance of game, this sauce can be prepared with wild duck, if available. The classic French addition of fruit cuts through the richness of the meat.

2 whole (double) duck breasts cut from 2 6-pound ducklings

SAUCE
2 ripe pears, peeled and cored
1 tsp mustard
1 cup Grand Marnier
1 cup clear honey

Preheat the oven to 420° F. Put the two duck breasts in a large baking pan and roast for about 30 minutes. Meanwhile, prepare the sauce. Purée the pears in a food processor or a blender with the mustard, Grand Marnier, and honey. Pour into a small pan and simmer for about 20 minutes. When the duck has cooked for 30 minutes, drain off the fat, place the duck breasts back in the pan and pour over the sauce. Lower the oven temperature to 400° F and bake for another 20 minutes. Skim any fat from the sauce and pour over the duck to serve. Serves 4.

CHAPTER FOUR

Vegetable Dishes and Accompaniments

Above: North Bridge at Concord, Massachusetts, where the first shots of the Revolution – "the shot heard round the world" – were fired.

*T*he staple crops learned about from the Native Americans – such as corn, beans, and squash – probably saved the lives of the early settlers in those first difficult years; to such an extent that they are now a part of the cooking heritage. Together with the potatoes, beets, and other farm crops and the mushrooms gathered from the wild, the range of vegetable dishes supports the wholesome approach to cooking so important in the region.

Right: Boston Baked Beans.

Red Bliss Potato Salad

Potatoes were a staple of the early settlers who would always cook them in their skins to avoid any waste.

3 pounds Red Bliss potatoes
2 Tbsps ground dill weed
1 tsp each salt and white pepper
1 Tbsp chopped fresh tarragon
2 cups sour cream
1 Tbsp chopped fresh parsley

Wash the potatoes and cut them into 1-inch cubes. Place in boiling, salted water and cook until just tender. Remove from the heat, drain and allow to cool. When the potatoes are cold, toss with the remaining ingredients and chill before serving. Serves 8.

Above right: preparing a meal on the Modern Glenwood stove.

Succotash

The Native Americans used to grow corn and beans together so that the corn stalks supported the bean crops. As they grew together, they were also cooked together, and given this wonderful name of succotash.

4 oz fresh lima beans
4 oz fresh green beans
4 oz fresh corn kernels
3 Tbsps butter
Salt and pepper
Chopped fresh parsley

Bring some water to a boil in a saucepan and add the lima beans first. After about 2 minutes, add the green beans. Follow these with the corn about 3 minutes before the end of cooking time. Drain and leave to dry.
Melt the butter in a saucepan and add the vegetables. Heat slowly, tossing or stirring occasionally, until heated through. Add salt and pepper to taste and stir in some chopped parsley. Serve immediately. Serves 6.

Scalloped Potatoes

Mashed or creamed potatoes were very much a favorite of the English settlers and often served with turkey.

2 pounds potatoes, peeled and quartered
Water to cover
¼ tsp salt
2 cups hot milk
2 Tbsps butter
Pinch of salt
Pinch of white pepper

Place the potatoes in a large pot, cover with water and add the ¼ tsp of salt. Cover the pot and bring to a boil. Cook for about 20-25 minutes or until tender. Drain well and return to the pot. Turn up the heat and mash the potatoes. When dry, add the hot milk and butter, beating it in well. Season with salt and pepper. Serves 8.

Boston Baked Beans

Because the Puritans did no work on Sundays, the women had to prepare two sets of meals for their hungry families on Saturdays. This dish became a particular favorite to leave on the hearth all day, ready for Saturday supper. Baked beans later became America's first "fast food." In winter months the cooked beans were tied in a muslin cloth and left outside to freeze. Bits could be broken off on a journey and quickly reheated to provide a hearty, warming meal.

1 pound dried navy beans
5 cups water
4 oz salt pork or slab bacon
1 onion
$\frac{1}{3}$-$\frac{1}{2}$ cup molasses
1 tsp dry mustard
Salt and pepper

Soak the beans overnight in the water. Transfer to fresh water to cover. Bring to a boil and allow to cook for about 10 minutes. Drain and reserve the liquid.
Preheat the oven to 300° F. Place the beans, salt pork or bacon and whole onion in a large, deep casserole or bean pot. Mix the molasses, mustard, salt and pepper with 1 cup of the reserved bean liquid. Stir into the beans and add enough bean liquid to cover all except the pork rind. Cover the casserole and bake in the oven for about 2 hours. Add the remaining liquid, stirring well, and cook another 1½ hours, or until the beans are tender. Uncover the beans for the last 30 minutes.
To serve, remove and discard the onion. Take out the salt pork or bacon and remove the rind. Slice or dice the meat and return to the beans. Check the seasoning and serve. Serves 6-8.

Fresh Creamed Mushrooms

1 pound even-sized chanterelle or button mushrooms
1 Tbsp lemon juice
2 Tbsps butter or margarine
1 Tbsp all-purpose flour
Salt and white pepper
¼ tsp freshly grated nutmeg
1 small bay leaf
1 blade mace
1 cup heavy cream
1 Tbsp dry sherry

Wash the mushrooms quickly and dry them well. Trim the stems level with the caps. Leave whole if small, halve or quarter if large. Toss with the lemon juice and set aside.
In a medium saucepan, melt the butter or margarine and stir in the flour. Cook, stirring gently, for about 1 minute. Remove from the heat, add the salt, pepper, nutmeg, bay leaf, and mace and gradually stir in the cream. Return the pan to the heat and bring to a boil, stirring constantly. Allow to boil for about 1 minute, or until thickened. Reduce the heat and add the mushrooms. Simmer gently, covered, for about 5 minutes, or until the mushrooms are tender. Add the sherry during the last few minutes of cooking. Remove the bay leaf and mace. Sprinkle with additional grated nutmeg before serving. Serves 4.

Harvard Beets

Serving beets as a hot vegetable rather than a salad ingredient is very much in the American tradition.

2 pounds small beets, trimmed
3 Tbsps cornstarch
½ cup sugar
Pinch of salt and pepper
1 cup dry white wine vinegar
¾ cup reserved beet cooking liquid
2 Tbsps butter

Place the beets in a large saucepan of water. Cover and bring to a boil. Lower the heat and cook gently until tender, about 30-40 minutes. Add more boiling water as necessary during cooking. Drain the beets, reserving the liquid, and allow the beets to cool.
When the beets are cool, peel them and slice into ¼-inch rounds, or cut into small dice. Combine the cornstarch, sugar, salt and pepper, vinegar, and the required amount of beet liquid in a large saucepan. Bring to a boil stirring constantly until thickened. Return the beets to the pan and heat through for about 5 minutes. Stir in the butter and serve immediately. Serves 6.

Right: tending the garden in the Pilgrim Village, a "living" museum in Plymouth, Massachusetts.

58

Chanterelle Omelet

Stuffed Acorn Squash with a Rum Glaze

The profitable Rhode Island rum trade of the eighteenth century led to many recipes that make use of this versatile spirit!

2 even-sized acorn squash
⅓ cup butter or margarine
2 cooking apples, peeled, cored, and cut into ½-inch pieces
½ cup pitted prunes, cut into large pieces
1 cup dried apricots, cut into large pieces
½ tsp ground allspice
6 Tbsps rum
½ cup chopped walnuts
½ cup golden raisins
½ cup packed light brown sugar

Preheat the oven to 350° F. Cut the squash in half lengthwise. Scoop out and discard the seeds. Place the squash skin side up in a baking dish with water to come halfway up the sides. Bake in the oven for about 30 minutes.
Melt half the butter in a saucepan and add the apples, prunes and apricots. Add the allspice and rum

Chanterelles, those very French mushrooms, are also frequently found growing wild in wooded areas in Vermont. Avoid washing them, since they absorb water. Just wipe them with damp paper towels if cleaning is necessary.

2 Tbsps butter
3 oz fresh chanterelle mushrooms, sliced
Salt and pepper
2 Tbsps finely chopped fresh parsley
3 eggs, at room temperature

Melt 1 Tbsp of the butter in a small pan. Sauté the mushrooms quickly, season with salt and pepper and add the chopped parsley. Set aside and keep them warm. Beat the eggs thoroughly with a fork or whisk in a small bowl. Place the remaining butter in an omelet pan and heat until foaming but not brown. Pour in the eggs and swirl over the bottom of the pan. Immediately stir the eggs with a fork to allow the uncooked mixture to run to the bottom of the pan. When the mixture is creamily set on top, scatter over the sautéed chanterelles and roll the omelet in the pan by flipping about a third of it to the middle and then flipping it out onto a hot plate. Serves 1.

and bring to a boil. Lower the heat and simmer gently for about 5-10 minutes. Add the nuts and golden raisins 3 minutes before the end of cooking time. Drain, reserving the liquid. Turn the squash over and fill the hollow with the fruit.
Melt the remaining butter in a saucepan and stir in the brown sugar. Melt slowly until the sugar forms a syrup. Pour on the fruit cooking liquid, stirring constantly. Bring back to a boil and cook until syrupy. Add more water if necessary. Spoon the glaze onto each squash, over the fruit, and cut edge. Bake for another 30 minutes, or until the squash is tender.
Serves 4.

Above left: a fruit and vegetable stall in Salem, Massachusetts.

Creamed Onions

Whole small onions in a creamy, rich sauce are part of Thanksgiving fare in Massachusetts, but they are too good to save for just once a year.

1 pound pearl onions
Boiling water to cover
2 cups milk
1 blade mace
1 bay leaf
2 Tbsps butter or margarine
2 Tbsps flour
Pinch of salt and white pepper
Chopped fresh parsley (optional)

Trim the root hairs on the onions but do not cut the roots off completely. Place the onions in a large saucepan and pour over the boiling water. Bring the onions back to a boil and cook for about 10 minutes. Transfer the onions to cold water, allow to cool completely and then peel off the skins, removing roots as well. Leave the onions to drain dry.

Place the milk in a deep saucepan and add the blade mace and the bay leaf. Bring just to a boil, take off the heat and allow to stand for 15 minutes.

Melt the butter in a large saucepan and, when foaming, stir in the flour. Strain on the milk, stirring well, and discard the bay leaf and mace. Bring to a boil and allow the sauce to simmer for about 3 minutes to thicken, stirring continuously. Add salt and white pepper to taste and stir in the onions. Cook to heat through, but do not allow the sauce to boil again. Serve immediately and garnish with chopped parsley, if desired. Serves 4.

Chestnut Stuffing

This delicious stuffing is the ideal accompaniment to the game birds and poultry so popular in New England.

8 oz dry chestnuts
1 quart warm water
8 oz dry white bread
2 cups chicken stock
4 Tbsps finely chopped onion
4 Tbsps finely chopped celery
2 Tbsps butter
2 tsps salt
½ tsp black pepper
¼ tsp poultry seasoning
¼ tsp sage
1 large egg

Cover the dry chestnuts with the water and soak overnight. The next day, simmer the chestnuts in the soaking water for 2 hours until tender, but not mushy. Preheat the oven to 325°F. Drain and cool the chestnuts, chop coarsely, and set aside.

Cube the bread and place in a large bowl. Soak in chicken stock and set aside. In a small skillet, sauté the onion and celery in the butter and add to the bread mixture. Add the seasonings and stir in the egg. Add the chestnuts and mix well. Place the stuffing in a greased ovenproof pan, and cook in the oven for 1 hour, or use to stuff a turkey, game bird, or chicken. Serves 8.

Above left: the Wright Tavern in Concord, Massachusetts, was taken as the headquarters of the British on April 19th 1775 after the first battle of the Revolutionary War at Lexington. Right: a lumber yard in Addison County, Vermont. The color of the fall leaves makes a pretty contrast to the snow covered ground and rooftops.

CHAPTER FIVE

Desserts, Pies, and Breads

Above: pretty covered bridges like this one at Stark are a common sight in New Hampshire.

*L*ike the rest of New England's cuisine, the origin of its sweet dishes is drawn from a variety of culinary influences, for example, many steamed and baked puddings stem from English recipes, while some rich cakes and pastries have obvious French origins. Traditional recipes were given a new twist once blended with local ingredients like cranberries, blueberries, pumpkins, and maple syrup. This created new recipes with a distinctly different accent – one that can be identified as New England to the core.

Right: Berkshire Apple Pancakes.

Blueberry Pie

Blueberries grow in abundance in the New England states and all over the country as well. Wild blueberries ripen in July, August, and September and are a real treat to look forward to.

2 quantities pastry for Pumpkin Pie recipe (see page 74)

(see page 74)

Corn Bread

Corn and cornmeal play a very important part in Massachusetts cuisine. Without the knowledge gained from the Native Americans on how to plant and grow corn, the people of the Massachusetts Bay Colony probably would not have survived their first winter.

10 whole eggs
1 cup sugar
1 Tbsp salt
1½ quarts milk
5⅔ cups cornmeal
7 cups bread flour
3 Tbsps baking powder
⅔ cup melted butter
½ tsp vanilla extract

Preheat the oven to 400°F. Beat the eggs, sugar, and salt until thick. Add the milk and sift in the cornmeal, bread flour, and baking powder. Add the melted butter and vanilla and stir in gently. Pour into a greased 24 × 8-inch baking pan. Bake for 25 minutes or until well risen and golden brown on top. Cool on a rack and cut into squares while still warm. Makes 24 squares.

FILLING

1 pound blueberries
2 Tbsps cornstarch
4 Tbsps water
2 Tbsps lemon juice
1 cup sugar
1 egg, beaten with a pinch of salt

Prepare the pastry in the same way as for the Pumpkin Pie recipe. Divide the pastry in half and roll out one half to form the base. Use a floured rolling pin to lower it into the dish, and press it against the sides. Chill the pastry in the dish and the remaining half of the pastry while preparing the filling.

Preheat the oven to 425°F. Place the fruit in a bowl and mix the cornstarch with the water and lemon juice. Pour it over the fruit, add the sugar, and mix together gently. Spoon the fruit filling into the pastry base. Roll out the remaining pastry on a lightly floured surface and cut it into strips. Use the strips to make a lattice pattern on top of the filling and press the edges to stick them to the pastry base. Cut off any excess pastry. Using your fingers or a fork, crimp the edges to decorate. Brush the crimped edge of the pastry and the lattice strips lightly with the beaten egg and bake in the oven for about 10 minutes. Reduce the heat to 350°F and bake for another 40-45 minutes. Serve warm or cold. Makes 1 pie.

Above left: a Shaker settlement.

Above: President Abraham Lincoln spent his vacations at Manchester, Vermont. The town had been decimated by the Civil War and benefited greatly from his visits, becoming a famous resort.

Steamed Cranberry Pudding

Colonial women brought their favorite recipes with them and learned to adapt them to the local produce, hence an English steamed pudding with American cranberries.

1½ cups all-purpose flour
2 Tbsps baking powder
Pinch of salt
1 cup chopped cranberries
1 small piece candied ginger, finely chopped
2 eggs, well beaten
½ cup clear honey
6 Tbsps milk

ORANGE SAUCE
Grated rind and juice of 1 orange
Grated rind and juice of ½ lemon
½ cup sugar
1 Tbsp cornstarch
¾ cup water
1 Tbsp butter or margarine

Sift the dry ingredients together in a large bowl. Toss in the cranberries and ginger. Mix the eggs, honey, and milk together and gradually stir into the dry ingredients and the cranberries. Do not over stir. The mixture should not be uniformly pink. The mixture should be of thick dropping consistency. Add more milk if necessary. Spoon the mixture into a well-greased pudding basin or bowl, cover with buttered foil and tie the top securely. Place the bowl on a rack in a pan. Add boiling water to come halfway up the sides of the basin. Cover the pan and steam the pudding for about 1½ hours, or until a skewer inserted into the center comes out clean. Leave to cool in the basin for about 10 minutes, loosen the edge with a knife and turn out onto a plate.

Meanwhile, place the orange and lemon rind and juice, the sugar, and cornstarch into a saucepan. Add the water, stirring to blend well. Bring to a boil and allow to simmer until clear. Beat in the butter or margarine and serve with the pudding. Serves 6.

Above left: cranberries are grown extensively in Massachusetts where the acidic peat soil is ideal for their cultivation. Although the first settlers used the wild berries widely in their cooking, it took over two hundred years to start their cultivation. Cranberry farming is now a big industry with hundreds-of-thousands of metric tons produced every year.

Berkshire Apple Pancakes

Apples were brought from the Old World, and these baked pancakes owe a lot both to German desserts and also French clafoutis.

2½ cups all-purpose flour
1¾ tsps salt
1¾ tsps sugar
1¾ tsps baking soda
1½ Tbsps baking powder
2 oz shortening
8 eggs
2½ cups buttermilk
1 Tbsp vanilla extract
1 tsp ground cinnamon
⅛ tsp ground nutmeg
2 Tbsps melted butter
3 large MacIntosh apples
Strawberry fans or orange twists to serve (optional)

GLAZE
4 Tbsps apple cider
2 Tbsps melted butter
½ cup dark brown sugar
¾ cup pure maple syrup

Combine all the dry ingredients and add the shortening, eggs, buttermilk, vanilla, cinnamon, nutmeg, and melted butter. With a wooden spoon, mix all the ingredients together. Do not over-mix; the mixture should look lumpy. Peel, core, and dice two of the apples and fold into the mixture. Allow to stand for 15 minutes before cooking. Preheat the oven to 375° F. Meanwhile, make the glaze. Combine the cider and butter over a low heat, add the sugar and maple syrup and mix well. Lightly brush 6 6-inch ovenproof French crêpe pans with softened butter. Heat in the oven for 3 minutes. Remove the pans from the oven and ladle into each about ¾ cup of batter, bringing it to within a ¼-inch of the top of the pans. Peel and core the remaining apple and cut into 24 slices, use to decorate the pancakes. Return to the oven for another 10 minutes Reduce the heat to 350° F and bake for 15-18 minutes, or until a skewer comes out clean from the center when tested. Remove from the oven and allow to stand for 5 minutes. Loosen the pancakes and slide out onto warmed plates. Lightly brush with glaze and serve the remaining glaze separately. Serve with a fruit decoration, if desired. The pancakes can also be prepared in one large skillet and sliced into wedges to serve. Serves 6.

Above left: a fascinating old photograph of a trader's stall in Faneuil Hall Market (also known as Quincy Market), Boston. Right: the Old Mill, in the historic town of Nantucket, Massachusetts, was built in 1746. Its milling machinery, made of wood, still works.

Maple Mousse

Johnnycakes

Native Americans made their corn bread by grinding corn, mixing it with water and baking it in a cake-like patty over a hot fire. These were known as Journey Cakes because they were easy to prepare when travelling, and somehow came to be called Johnnycakes.

1 cup cornmeal
1 tsp salt
1 tsp sugar
1¼ cups water

Mix the cornmeal, salt, and sugar together in a bowl. Boil the water and beat in gradually until the batter is smooth, but very thick (it may not be necessary to add all the water). Drop spoonfulls onto a well greased, hot griddle and fry over medium heat for 6 minutes. Turn over and cook on the other side for 5 minutes. Serve immediately. Serves 6.

Refined from the sap of the sugar maple tree, maple is the finest of all syrups. Don't be tempted to use substitutes in this rich mousse; that would never be Vermont style!

1 cup Grade A Vermont maple syrup
6 egg yolks
1½ cups heavy cream

In a saucepan, bring the maple syrup to boiling point and cook rapidly to reduce from 1 cup to ¾ cup. Be careful not to let the syrup burn. Meanwhile, in a stainless steel bowl, whip the egg yolks until foamy. Pour the hot reduced maple syrup slowly over the beaten egg yolks, whipping constantly. Continue whipping the mixture until cool. In a separate bowl, whip the heavy cream until stiff. Fold the cream gently into the mousse mixture and pour into a chilled bowl. Refrigerate until set and serve chilled. Serves 4-6.

Above left: traditional Shaker dress and artifacts can be seen on permanent display at the Shaker settlement at Enfield, New Hampshire.

Fresh Raspberries with Cream

Fresh berries at their peak can be served in the simplest way.

3 cups fresh raspberries or a combination of different berries
1½ cups fresh heavy cream

Select the raspberries or other berries as fresh as possible. Look over and discard any bruised or damaged berries. Rinse only if absolutely necessary. Arrange the berries carefully in stemmed glass dessert dishes. Drizzle each serving with heavy cream and serve. Serves 6.

Pumpkin Pie

The origins of this recipe can be traced back to East Anglia in Great Britain. The recipe was brought over with the Pilgrim Fathers and was served at the first dinner of Thanksgiving in 1621. Spices were not included, though, until the clipper ships began their trade. In the Southern states, squash is often used as an alternative ingredient, but whichever you choose, Thanksgiving would not be the same without it.

PASTRY
1 cup all-purpose flour
Pinch salt
¼ cup butter, margarine, or shortening
Cold milk, to mix

FILLING
1½ cups cooked and mashed pumpkin
1 cup milk
½ cup brown sugar
1 tsp ground cinnamon
½ tsp ground ginger
¼ tsp grated nutmeg
2 eggs
Whipped Cream, to serve

To prepare the pastry, sift the flour and salt into a mixing bowl. Rub in the fat until the mixture resembles bread crumbs. Stir in enough cold milk to bring the mixture together into a firm ball. Cover and chill for about 30 minutes. Preheat the oven to 425°F. Roll the pastry out on a floured surface and use to line a 10-inch pie dish. Line with baking paper and fill with dried beans, rice, or pasta. Bake in the oven for 10 minutes then remove from the oven and take out the beans and paper. Reduce the oven temperature to 375°F and return the crust to the oven for another 5-10 minutes, or until it is pale brown. Raise the oven temperature to 400°F. Place all the filling ingredients, except the eggs, into the top of a double boiler. Over boiling water, bring the mixture just to scalding point. In a bowl, beat the eggs until frothy. Stir a small amount of the hot mixture into the eggs and return the egg mixture to the rest of the hot pumpkin. Stir continuously over a gentle heat until the mixture begins to thicken. Pour the mixture into the baked pie shell. Bake the pie in the oven for about 30 minutes, or until the filling sets and a knife tip inserted into the center of the filling comes out clean. Serve slightly warm with whipped cream. Makes 1 10-inch pie.

Above left: costumed staff portraying colonial life in the Pilgrim Village at Plymouth, Massachusetts.

Steamed Brown Bread

This is the classic accompaniment to one of Boston's famous dishes – baked beans. It's traditional to cook it in a can. The raisins are optional.

1 cup fine cornmeal
1 cup wholewheat flour
1 cup rye flour
1½ tsps baking soda
1 tsp salt
1 cup seedless raisins, chopped
¾ cup dark molasses
2 cups buttermilk

Sift the dry ingredients into a large bowl and return the bran to the bowl. Add the raisins and mix to distribute. Mix the molasses, and buttermilk together. Make a well in the center of the flour and pour in the mixture. Mix just until well blended. Grease 2 tall 1-pound coffee cans and pour the batter in. Cover the tops with greased foil and tie on with string. Place the cans on a rack in a deep saucepan. Pour enough boiling water around the cans to come about halfway up the sides. Allow the water to bubble gently to steam the bread for 2-3 hours in the covered pan. Add more boiling water as necessary during cooking. The bread is ready when a skewer inserted into the center of the bread comes out almost clean. Invert the cans on to a wire rack to cool. Makes 2 1-pound loaves.

Above right: delivery wagons collected outside the bakery on Albany Street in Roxbury, Massachusetts.

Above: a traditional wood-fired pottery kiln is used in Old Sturbridge Village, Massachusetts, where a traditional early nineteenth-century community has been re-created.

Maple Walnut Bread

One whole cup of maple syrup gives a true Vermont taste to this quick bread. The orange juice adds a fresh tang. This bread is better if 'ripened' for at least one day before eating.

2 Tbsps melted butter
1 cup Vermont maple syrup
1 egg, well beaten
Grated rind of 1 lemon
2½ cups all-purpose flour
3 tsps baking powder
½ tsp baking soda
¼ tsp salt
¾ cup walnuts, chopped (3 reserved whole for decoration)
¾ cup orange juice

Preheat the oven to 250°F. Blend the butter, maple syrup, egg, and lemon rind in a bowl until creamy. In a separate bowl, sift the dry ingredients together and add the nuts. Combine the two mixtures alternately with the orange juice. Spoon into a greased loaf pan and bake in the oven for 1 hour or until a skewer inserted into the center of the loaf comes out clean. Cool the loaf on a wire rack. After the bread cools, glaze with more maple syrup and put the reserved walnuts on top. Best served the day after baking. Makes 1 loaf.

Spiced Cranberry Nut Bread

Sassamanesh was the colorful Native American name for this equally colorful berry which grew wild in Massachusetts. Not restricted to culinary usage, it was also employed in fabric dying and the healing of wounds.

2 cups all-purpose flour
1 tsp baking powder
1 cup sugar
1 tsp baking soda
Pinch of salt
$\frac{1}{4}$ tsp nutmeg
$\frac{1}{4}$ tsp ginger
$\frac{1}{2}$ cup orange juice
2 Tbsps butter or margarine, melted
4 Tbsps water
1 egg
1 cup fresh cranberries, roughly chopped
1 cup hazelnuts, roughly chopped

Preheat the oven to 325° F. Sift the dry ingredients and spices into a large mixing bowl. Make a well in the center and pour in the orange juice, melted butter or margarine, water, and egg. Using a wooden spoon, beat the liquid mixture, gradually drawing in the flour from the outside edge. Add the cranberries and nuts and stir to mix completely.
Lightly grease a loaf pan about 9×5 inches. Press a strip of wax paper on the base and up the sides. Lightly grease the paper and flour the whole inside of the pan. Spoon or pour in the bread mixture and bake in the oven for about 1 hour, or until a skewer inserted into the center of the loaf comes out clean. Remove from the pan, carefully peel off the paper, and cool on a wire rack. Lightly dust with powdered sugar, if desired, and cut into slices to serve. Makes 1 loaf.

Pumpkin Bread

You'll find pumpkin in many New England recipes. In this quick bread, it adds moisture and a beautiful color.

1 cup canned pumpkin
2 eggs
Scant $\frac{1}{2}$ cup shortening, melted
2 cups all-purpose flour
$\frac{3}{4}$ cup sugar
$\frac{1}{4}$ tsp ground cinnamon
$\frac{1}{4}$ tsp grated nutmeg
$\frac{1}{8}$ tsp ground cloves
1 tsp baking soda

Preheat the oven to 350° F. Mix the pumpkin, eggs, and shortening together well and sift in the dry ingredients. Fold together and put into a well greased loaf pan. Bake for 1 hour or until a knife inserted into the center of the bread comes out clean. Makes 1 loaf.

Apple Crisp

Apple crisp is an old-fashioned dessert that has remained immensely popular over the years.

6-8 tart apples
$\frac{1}{2}$ cup granulated sugar
$\frac{1}{4}$ tsp ground cloves
$\frac{1}{2}$ tsp ground cinnamon
2 tsps lemon juice

TOPPING
$\frac{3}{4}$ cup all-purpose flour
6 Tbsps butter
$\frac{1}{2}$ cup brown sugar

Cream or vanilla ice cream to serve

Preheat the oven to 350° F. Peel and slice the apples. Blend the remaining ingredients and toss with the apples to mix thoroughly. Pour into a greased 1½-quart casserole. Blend the topping ingredients together into a crumbly consistency and sprinkle over the top of the apples. Bake for 45 minutes or until the apples are tender and the top is brown and crisp. Serve with cream or vanilla ice cream. Serves 4-6.

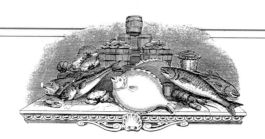

Index

PICTURE CREDITS

Historical photographs pages 1, 6 (William T. Clark), 10, 18 (H. P. Macintosh), 20, 24, 26, 36, 40 (Fred Quimby), 44, 56 (Mary Northend), 60, 70, and 76, courtesy of the Society for the Preservation of New England Antiquities. "Family Picnic" page 30, and "Boston Cooking School" page 50, courtesy of the Boston Athenaeum.

ACKNOWLEDGMENTS

The publishers would like to thank home economist Sue Philpot and stylist Blake Minton for their contribution to the photographs on pages 2-3, and the front cover.